OUTLAW BLUE

PIMPS, POETS, AND PREACHERS

New and Selected Poems by

Justin Booth

Outlaw Blue: Pimps, Poets & Preachers

Copyright © August 2016 by Justin Booth

Cowboy Buddha Publishing, LLC

No part of this book may be reproduced or transmitted in any form or by any means, electronic or mechanical, including photocopy, recording, or any information storage or retrieval system, without permission in writing from the author or his agents, except by a reviewer to be printed in a magazine or newspaper, or electronically transmitted on radio or television.

ISBN 978-0-9856076-7-8

Cover & Book Design by Jessica Dyer

Illustrations by Justin Booth

Publishing Logo by Ted Nichols

Cowboy Buddha Publishing, LLC

Benton, Arkansas

Table of Contents

Crossroad	1
Hurt by Everything I Believe	6
Short Hair	8
Groovy	10
Pffff	11
She Knows	14
Bad Bitch Muse	18
Wishes	20
His Poems	23
I'd Never	27
Open Campus Kids	31
Chewing Things Over	33
Dirt Road Cultures	35
Call Me A Cab	38
On Sundays	40
There Are Poems	42
Thank You	44
Book of Numbers	46
Good Morning	51
Bedtime Stories	54
Game	57
Move Slow	59
Still	63

Everybody Loved Her Grandpa	66
Poor Baby	73
She's Gone to Texas	75
Second Life	77
Sadder Than Pablo	79
Before the Poem	82
Sunrise At Sunset	85
Love Me Tender	88
Second Hand Sheep	91
Poetry Saves	92
Start Again	93
Sorry	95
Children Together	98
My Coffee Outdoors	101
Cheese and Whine	102
I See	104
Words Among Us	109
Undone	114
Maybe Better	120
Them Bones	124
Dream Lovers Die	127
Prayer	128

For my muse.

Crossroad

She smoked
long cigarettes
enjoyed
a boxed wine
and
didn't hesitate
to drop the
f -bomb
for the sake
of a laugh.

She worked
her ass off
days then nights
to get by,
surprised late
with the
beautiful baby
boy who

would one
day dance
on tables at
Vino's with
a brokedown
man given
second chance.

She was proud,
as a little girl,
of her badge
and blue uniform
father who
seemed to know
everybody
and all the
hookers by
name.

She was a
crooked stem

desktop lamp
in a dark
storyteller's
room,
the only one
who could
make him see
that hate was
not
the answer
to a love
unreturned.

She is tears
in the night,
and hands
held tight
over ears,
trying to ignore
the ghost
voices that

say she
is not enough.

The voices
from within
that tell her
she will
never be
enough.

She is a
niggling itch,
a constant
reminder of
a strong proud
southern girl,
that I do
not
deserve,
a desire unfulfilled-

I want her so.

I told her
once
that she might
be the one,

she said
get a job

we are at
the crossroads
still.

Hurt by Everything I Believe

I forgave her,
I guess
more important
she forgave me

for my lack
of graceful behavior
at the inevitable
end but

I never forgave
that short self-loving
preacher that was
so jealous of me.

I didn't forgive god.

I wont. Fuck him,
I'd rather be in hell

than work
his corners anymore.

Oh I believe still,
but fuck him.
God or not loyalty
is a two way street.

He is just a broke ass pimp
dancing with old ladies who
have given up on their dreams,
but I will always be true blue,

and the most desperate,
 can count on me.
Always.
My actions not bullshit talk.

Short Hair

You're gonna
learn how to
mind your
fucking business,
deuce up,
and stand still
during count.

If you don't
make a calender
or let anybody
put a steering wheel
on your back,

one day

that big grey door
will buzz and
open up and

you'll go back
to the world and
women will
sleep with you
sometimes
just because you
were a con.

It's gonna be o.k.
- this is my fucking house.

Groovy

I'm not
saying that
smoking weed and
a long afternoon

talking art

with a great looking
young lady will
cure depression,

I'm just saying
it makes the
transition into

mania

a little more
groovy is all.

Pffff

I don't like it,
I said, as a child.
Her eyebrows
did a thing like
your hands do,
when you drink
from a stream.
You think I did,
pfff,
I waited through
the one, then you
lived with the other.

We started meeting
for a beer before
church, until the
shushing, then
just beers,

I danced on Vino's
tables with her
five year old.

We both had a
past but we made
a deal only to
do bad at the D.

We would tell
each other when
we started to get
wierd but the
timing was too
close, now a
great scar on
my chest, she just
took off her
heart vest but

timing is everything.

We both still wake,
the sun continues
to bounce itself alive
each day new hope.

All I know is
I love that crazy
girl, and I've put
in my time
to see what happens

next.

She Knows

Once she read
to me,
like story time
only better, the
most beautiful girl
in the world.

Something sad,
yet funny,
and quirky but good.
She read of
raindrops bruising
flower petals.
I watched her
read, the way
her lips shaped
the words her
expression framed
each mood.

She knows
I love her.

She watches me
sometimes with
eyes more amazing
than any seven
things ever,
present or past.
She looks at me
and her eyes that
whisper passages
in French about
love making
hold me rapt.
I do not speak
French but crave her
attentions sans pudeur

and she knows.

A pretty girl took
her away to sleep
under electric blankets
and watch movies
about other times
and loves.
Chick porn I say,
and she laughs
tells the pretty girl
that only
porn is porn
but chick flicks
are great too.
I begin writing
this poem as
they leave me.

She knows no one
will ever see it.

I share her love

with another and
ours is the one held
quiet as sin.
I love her
silent and secret.
It is enough
for me that

she knows.

Bad Bitch Muse

No secret
I guess I
crush

on the most
beautiful
ones, the
badass chicks,
tatted and turnt.

I'm kinda a
poet, it's kinda
my job.

Surely it wasn't
her last name

really

but she really
was darling.

When I wanted
a picture
she proved me
a creep.

It's just the
attention
I need anyway.

I still
write her
poems.

Wishes

I wish you
had money,
she said
pausing the
Youtube
beauty tutorial
and smiled an
apple extending
smile tempting
Grace.

You mean you
wish your
sugar daddy
wasn't some
broke ass
nobody knows
him poet.

I just know
you'd buy me
things
if you had
money.

Yes was all
he said,
if I weren't
a poet,
silently implied.

She sat Indian
style in the living
room floor,
cut-off shorts and
a Keep Austin
Wierd tank top,
practiced
putting on
midnight eyes

and matte liquid
lips made,
it seemed,
for kissing.

And she was a woman.
And she was art.

An object of beauty.
A being full of life.
And he thought
I wish I had money
I'd write poems
for you every night
and you'd forever
be art.

His Poems

The way
he flicked gently
open his late
Grandfather's
chunky Zippo-

its finish worn
and polished
by the fine
Delta dirt
and overall
pocket
of a man
who climbed
daily
on and off
a red Farmall
tractor-

the way he
drew deeply
on the hand
fashioned
cigarette,
breathing
out a great cloud
then still
allowing the last
slender bit
of smoke to
escape gently
from his nostrils.

It was
the way he
dropped his chin
and pushed back
his hair
up and straight out
and gave a

well rehearsed
cutting up of his eyes
the way a
boy might
when he first
wooed his
mother.

The women that
he had been with,

the drugs
and the booze,
and prisons
and jails,

and
the women-

this last one
most of all.

This was
the tragedy
he wrote.

These were
his poems.

His work,
then,
that of recorder
of the
melancholy
life
he had created.

I'd Never

I remember
once when
I would never
grow old,
so many
years ago
now.

Just being grown
seemed so
many miles
from that FHA
house in Caraway
on cemetery road.

That was Then,
and Rumblefish,
a full set of
Worldbooks from

1976, and a
black and white
set out back,
beside my
roll-away bed.

Life's lesson,
love doesn't last
and a marriage,
a move, and
a new home.
I remember
when Jonesboro
seemed so large.

I remember
when I
could not die.
I pulled back
scarlet swirls
and pushed

them in again.
I rode on top,
outside of cars.

I carried
my big brothers
.22 pistol
tucked in my
waistband,
the grip was
small and branded
with a buffalo.

Wind rushed
through my hair,
and dope
through the rest,
at some point then,
feeling alone.

I remember

finding a wife,
building a home,

I remember
when my daughters
still spoke
to me.

I remember rehabs,
and prisons, and
life on the streets-
a cardboard sign
and spare change.

I remember.

I remember once,
I would never grow old.

Open Campus Kids

I want a burger
from the Dog,
with too much
mustard and onions,
and a Big K cola
to wash it down.

I want to stand
around the side after
and burn one
with those people
I used to go there
with, the people
from Nettleton High.

I want to be teen
sure
about everything
and nothing

but just
for a moment.

Just for a little,
I'd like to be young.

Chewing Things Over

Cold-steel
and gun-oil
flavored
chewing gum.

Big seller
during
the holidays.
Last ditch ideas
from an age
where
the attempts
are mostly about
the selfie
but the quiet
dead
numbers growing
are about escape
from head

and home.

From heart.

Tattooed
suicide girls
blowing bubbles
and then POP!

What?
It's a lock,
and silent night
for the others
left to deal.

Dirt Road Cultures

The songs of
my childhood
are snaggle-toothed
pony-tailed
girls skipping
rope on packed-dirt
playgrounds and
ready-or-not
here-I-come
near dusk,
sultry summers
in Arkansas.
Later locust's
chants through
window screens
and chicken-frying
grease popping
in the kitchen.

The stories are
Jesus and Superman,
Robin Hood and Zorro.
But also Boogerman Jenkins
and Grandpa
versus the utility-pole
people who
wanted to rape
his farm,
boogering
him in the process,
his pride.
My great-uncle
paying the black kids
in Blythesville
to dance for him.

Some childhood
stories are secret.

My paintings,

sandy bean fields,
cotton patches,
sunsets and cypress
grey barns.
Bono bridge,
still life, landscapes
stuff like that.

Tattoos of pretty
girls on old men's arms.
Decoration day.

Art in my early years,
everywhere I looked.

Call Me a Cab

They say
that he walked
naked
into the desert
and tried to climb
onto the wing
of a taxiing
aircraft after success
blew his mind.

Hopper, I mean.

What was the
plane doing out there
anyway?

They say it made
some top 5 list.
Breakdowns.

Hollywood.
Go ahead and see.

I thought they
said taxi.

On Sundays

There is an angel
in Long Island
who prays for
me like my
mama always has.

The wife of a
poet friend
with devils
I guess just
like mine.

Demons of
her own once,
I'm told,
then loosed.
Her spirit burned
bright driving
shadows and

darkness.

Now they go
to church together

and this lady
from up North
in Long Island she
prays for me

on Sundays

like my woman
used to do
before I fell
from grace.

There Are Poems

There are poems

like ex-lovers
who met
me
where I was,
at certain
moments in
time.
The poems
perfect and
satisfying
in my
circumstance
as I read
them.
Like ex-wives,
some of them
are no longer

in my life,
I wish
them well
but no longer
have place for
them.
People
and poetry
come in and
go back out

(again)

of our lives
for a reason.

Thank You

I know
I have been
hateful
to you.
I was lost
in my
passion.
The truth
is
I miss you
very much.
I probably
should
thank you
for
making me
alive again
to love.
Thank you

for
making me
desirable again
to women.
I should thank you
for the
unrequited
love that
warmed
my bones
again
for a while.
Thank you.

Book of Numbers

Two-faced is
the name she called,
curse your god and
kill yourself.

Three days and six
into relapse and
spiraling down
we were newly wed,
she was an angelic child
of Billy Burroughs and
kicking against the goads.

Forty days, no more,
since we had stolen
away from rehab,
the exodus,
our hearts hardened
and necks stiff,

willing sacrifices
on blood stained alter,
but today our worship
offered no respite.

Tears fat as Martha's
rolled down her cheeks
leaving Revlon tracks,
ashes and sack-clothe.
Unable to wash away
born-again
dope-sick Jones.
I offered no comfort,
instead righteous indignation,
I lashed out.

A paired countenance?
Truly that and more.
Ten Thousand faces
I have known.
A Thousand Thousand

lies, to keep us high.

The number of
finger and thumb
rolled cotton balls
dried stiff,
orange caps and
rigs dulled and
matchbook sharpened
with the units
worn smooth on
over-used barrels
left behind busted-up-dressers,
pay-by-the-week motels,
without end,
like Abraham's children.

Numbers this great
have names known
only to the church
of long dead magicians-

earliest mathematicians,
hookah and hashish,
bridging the gap
between sand and stars,
between Heaven and Earth.

Each face, each place and
infinite next pilgrim
share singular purpose-

a prayerful look forward.

Scanning without cease
the horizons, the very
edge of paradise,
hungry eyes searching
(milk and honey I promise)
through tunnel vision slits
of unending masks
seeking favor, discernment and grace-
forgiveness for sins as yet uncopped and

the darkest spirit asking me,
in a small still voice,

Good and faithful servant
who will you be in this moment
in order to stay loaded today?

Good Morning

We woke
early
evacuating
slots
on asphalt,
lined reflective
yellow,
each man
parked
for the night-
smothering
Arkansas summers.

Winters we slept
in doorways
and on landings,
storm and shelter,
that sort of thing.
When the first city
bus moved from

shop to depot,
when the first
stinking trucks
snatched and
dumped green dumpsters
we were already
gone- making way

for citizens
whose jobs were
downtown.

Buckshot and Tommy
would go to the Sally,
cold coffee and grits.
Tramp met a guy
at the corner and
hopped into his truck.
Three dollar hammer
and cloth nail bag in hand.
I walked each day
to Mom's Liquor on Main,

then spent 5th floor days
with Hank, and Beat kids
and Ray Carver poems.

And 2nd floor pecking
out words of my own.

This morning after
the song birds and breakfast-

fresh juice and prosciutto with cheese-

and all I could think was
I guess I should vacuum the pool.

then

things always change,
nothing lasts forever,
no matter how good or how bad.

Bedtime Stories

Never resting,
in those days,
in those places
sleep was
a pretty girl
playing
at hard to get.

When you see
us chin on chest
in parks or
wobbly-necked
in air-conditioned
public spaces
it is hard not
to count us lazy.

We never rest
even if we sleep.

And each one
of us courts
the pretty girl.
We want her.
She offers us peace.

Some with brown
bottles, others
with black-bottomed
spoon and I as often
as anyone.

I told myself stories
and poems.

Bedtime stories.
I wrote another world.

I dreamed of relevance.

Interviews on art, poetry, romance.

I live my dreams now.

I saw Carlos
stretched out
on a pallet
behind the old
Veterans Center

yesterday

and I think
how lucky that
I am rested
and still have a shot
at being relevant.

Game

The guy drilling
Old E into my
chest lost his mama
and grandma
in one crazy
BANG
moment and he got
blamed.

He don't
give a fuck about
no outlaw.

And the Cheshire girls
with their sexy lips
disappear just like
they're supposed to do.

The keyboards are

quieter now but
never still.
and still you fear it.

And guys like Knute Rockne
or Dan Gables or
Brian Robinson in my
own fight,
the greatest coaches say
envision the win.

I learn from the loss,
pick at the carnage
for arts sake,
I remember the jones,

but I picture the win,
keep pecking away,

because the only victory
in this game is relevance.

Move Slow

In the places
I have lived
lives, nine
times ninety,
the places and
the lives
numbers that
shame felines,
(The things
that I have done.
the same feelings,
shame.)
in these places
things move
slow.
Slow as steam
from a gut-pile
left hunter fresh
on November

mornings
in Arkansas woods.
Slow as crows
feast, for thanksgiving
until no evidence
remains.
At nineteen,
up North with
an uncle,
days spent
breaking back
and mopping
hot tar
I learned this
most valuable
lesson of all
in a bar called
Lost Acres
outside of Chicago,
on the Joliett side.
I met a guy

named Lucky
he had white hair,
a quick grin
and a small fleet
of trucks.
He rode a
Knucklehead Harley,
was clever,
and smooth with
ladies. He was
everything
I had always
pretended to be.
Lucky moved slow.
He took me
to King's Shoeshines,
hooked me up
with dark ladies
whose tits
had cost more
than my car,

he drove me to
Cicero and showed
me where
to cop dope.
The first bag
on him.
The lesson
didn't stick though
until he asked
a pistol favor,
my debt weighing
heavy in hand.
In moments
like these
things move slow,
because you
don't just ask
a guy
to kill someone
all at once.

Still

Mom used to
step on
the chocolate
milk.

She would
every once
in a great while
buy a
half a gallon
of store brand
chocolate
milk-

no bunnies
or zany cowboy
logos at
extra cost-

then she'd
refill the gallon
of "white"
milk, pour
the sweet treat
over a half
gallon plain
making it
less rich.
No less tasty.

Mama had 6 kids,
watched nickels
and dimes.

She stepped on
the milk but
I never got
used to it
any other way.

I drink it
that way
still.

Everybody Loved Her Grandpa

Her pockets
weren't the only
things that had
been high
in Nashville,
living
mood to mood
with a pimp
son of a ton
of great songs
and that one
from the radio.

His chip bigger
than his shoulders
maybe a little
greater
than his talent.

No,

she'd been
junkie angels
high,
and front yard
crying low.

She'd mostly
come back,
crashing hard,
but walking
away from the
landing-
they say
that makes
it a good one.

He was not in
better shape, and
truth told a

little crazy,

still,

for dope and booze
and the records
of her former
Harlem River
Daddy, her other
favorites too.

She'd made it back,
had to get back,
down to Arkansas
back to the farm.

He dropped in there,
traveling from
the last place to
anyplace next,
a big shot

without a single
dollar bill.

They took a ride
down back roads,
the trash in the
floorboards
ankle deep.
She drank her
last beer.
He smoked
a cashed bowl.

They bragged
about scars,
laughed like
they'd never seen
death eating crackers-
the shake
and bake kids-
and famine

eating the rest
of them,
its teeth deep
and drawing back
blood
before pushing in.

Then they talked
small voiced
about ones who
didn't come
down,
buried in boxes,
in worm
riddled ground.

When their time
was done they
never noticed,
counting out change
at the Legion,

ordered two more
cheap beers.

They huddled
and chuckled and
shed half a tear,
but everybody
knew they were
too much alike

to be real.

So instead
she hugged his
neck and said
again soon,
but he was
already writing
a sad story
in his head.

And she was
just like her
Grandpa,
and he was just
like everybody
else.

Poor Baby

Too sad
for poetry.
Too far gone
to save.
Even the dogs
distance
themselves and
the cat just
howls
for a leveling
of his bowl.

I cannot paint,
and prose sounds
dumb, and the
stage it seems
is for those
much prettier than me.

I am lost
in selfish introspection.

I am too
sad to write
a poem.

She's Gone to Texas

Carrie brought
another round,
scolded Ethan

gently

and left.
Boots watched

as she made
her way
between tables

in her
friendly manner.

"I don't
get
you two"

"Simple"

Blue said
without
looking up,

"She likes
the way I talk
but hates
the things I say."

Second Life

I'm afraid
I've gotten fat,
my face like
yesterday's mirror
covered in scars
and lines.

When I say
I like the young
girls,
I mean thirty-five
and then
hypothetically-
I'm not really
a closer.

The most outlaw
thing I have done
all day is talking
too loud at Dizzy's

about the shit
I used to do-

dope and
hustlin' and
that time I fought
that guy in prison-
started before he knew
I left him sitting
on the toilet his
pants around his
ankles; he never saw
it coming.

Quiet she said,
and freshened my
drink, and I think
about how lucky-

some days I don't even
mind the blue skies.

Sadder Than Pablo

The train
droned
on, close
but too far
to see.
The house fly
gestured like
an evil genius,
hatching
doomsday plans
then bowing
his head
and praying
before drinking
from the ring,
wet and clear-
a sweating
beer can
footprint on

an end table
left over
from somebody
else's life.
A murder of
crows cry
foul, then leap.
A new rush
of wings, one
peels away then
lights gently
as night, on
a chimney
gone cold.

"Did you used
to know her?"

"Not anymore."

"Mmm."

The fly buzzed
away so that
the can might
land,
and she wished
she'd
never asked.

Before The Poem

He thought
about the things
he had known,
and the people.
About the time
when he was sixteen
when his mother
found the candle stub
and black bent spoon
in his dresser drawer.
About the girl
from St Louis who
had broken his heart,
then the other
who had broken
his heart and
gone to St Louis.
He thought about
reading aloud

to his children
all that time ago,
and time
on the streets
not so long ago.
He thought about
the first time
he walked down the
corridor of county jail
in the early morning hours
because that's when
they take you to prison.
He thought of Lil' Black,
standing at his own
barred cell door
in his boxers shouting
"I'm Stick Booth"
over and over
until the whole felony side,
all three cell blocks,
was chanting it

over and over
like a cheer at 4 a.m..
He thought of his children,
and the kids he had chosen.
All of this,
more,
he thought about
before drinking his drink
and letting his fingertips
land
angel and pinhead
on the keyboard,
over and over
until he could
no longer stand
to think.

Sunrise at Sunset

Breaking rays
in soldiers ranks
invade Mother's
living room
having conquered
Venetian blind.

I sit quiet
as can,

she'll get up
when she hears.

She needs
her rest.

My morning drink
the instant,
her machine is broken

she'd given it up.

I am
surrounded

by
the past.

Trinkets of
yesterday.

Bucktoothed photos,
a painting by Lisa,
and Grandma's
salt and pepper
shakers bang drums
of dark skinned
children.

My biggest
fear is

that one
of us

will go
first.

Love Me Tender

Me and Baby
pull into a
convenience store
with a sign
hawking
fountain drinks
and Chicken
"Love me"
tenders.

I am pumping
gas when a
drop-top Camaro
pulls in and
a golden-skinned
pretty boy
with jewelry,
long hair and a beard
jumps out

and floats
to the entrance
smart phone in
his whistling
hands.

The pump kicks
off and me and
baby and
the beardo are
all back inside
our cars.

Jesus Christ
in a convertable I say.

No George Harrison.

Too gawdy,
I say,
George wouldn't

be caught dead
in a car like

that.

Second Hand Sheep

In the footpad's hour
between discount tricks
and newspapers tossed,
I am troubled
at the ghost of you.
Memories of when
I fooled myself.

All other time is lost.

In these hours
of utter abandon,
of madness
and indecision-
I live every moment
 again and again

counting seconds
as sheep
and passing out drunk
as sleep.

Poetry Saves

Donnie killed Verless
and I
call Stick
True Blue.

I don't know
if he can

DO IT

without the booze,

" Ethan wept."

but I'll kill myself
on the Cross
of Creek and Coke
and rise again
before I'm done.

For you.

Start Again

In dim morning
light I saw
her.

My first cup,
my father's day,
the heater kicked
off then a sigh.

She was like Charlotte
suspended it seemed
by single unseen
tether.

I stopped there,
where she was backlit.
Morning sun, grey,
through the sheers
then her.

I watched.

Coffee cooling.

In jerking
start-stop movement
she suddenly began
her descent.

Two thoughts-

when did I quit
being amazed
at such things?

thank goodness
I started again.

Sorry

Some of them
actually
loved me.

I am sorry
most of all
for that.

Lynne might have
if I had let her,
I think Kara did.

Gina never
had a chance.

I was too
afraid.

Some of them

loved the idea
of a man who
would turn his
back on God.
Blame him
for the girl who
sang his songs.

One asked
what does she
have
that I
don't.

She would stare
at the photos
framed on my wall
and say,

am I not
as pretty?

don't I
love art?

do I not
do the things
you craved her
to do?

She loved me

and for that
I am sorriest
of all.

Children Together

If we were children
together on some
playground of a
made up world
I would show
out for you-
turning somersaults
as I vaulted from
a pinnacle swing,
loosing slack-
jaggling chains
to twist behind me.
My rubber soled
Keds smacking down
solid on hard packed
dirt. I would cut my
eyes to see if you saw
from a teetering
tottered board

lifting you up
gloriously.

I would share my
lemon-heads with you,
my red-hots, I'd
give you the arrowhead
my brother gave me-
a treasure that is
the finest that I
might own, I
imagine you'd like
it quite a lot. I would
woo you with notes that
said check yes or no,
and if you said yes
I'd run slower
at kiss chase in your honor.

I would stretch
out long and lean

in hot, spring-sun warmed
fields of clover looking
for the lucky one that
would make you
grow old with me.

If we were children
together I would love
you nearly as much
as I do right now.

My Coffee Outdoors

I like when
the humming bird
sits still
just a moment

unflapped

by the world,
then
is gone again,
ambition restored.

Cheese and Whine

My children
just left for
the school bus.

One of them
was crying
about cheese.

I promise you
I was the coolest
chick in high school.

Well not the
most popular or
prettiest maybe.

But I have always
thought my own
thoughts.

I didn't have
this style yet, no
horn rimmed glasses-

that rainbow dress
not even a thought.
But I promise I was

wild inside, oh
the things I did
in high school.

My children
just caught
the school bus.

One of them
crying
for cheese.

I See

We all keep our
eye to the peephole.

Cookies are the
business cards of
our 5 and Dimes.

Brick and mortar
slain like the
buffalo on the
plains.

In this age
I buy books
and boots,
jerk off to
electronic boobs
I tweet
and they swoon.

I keep my eye
for an eye
to the peephole
for a peephole.

I let them see.

They see
the scars
and the vomit,
boogers and
Hep C.

They see
the ugliest part
of me,
if they put
an eye to
the peephole.

Fair exchange

because I see
the daughters
of dozens of dads
smile at my words
and warm
my old broken heart.

I see jazzmen
in Ireland
Travis picking
hillbilly tunes,
the songs of my father
and theirs.

I see stylized motifs,
India's truck art,
beautiful work
by Haider Ali,
and her street markets
with colors just

as rich.

I peek into the most
intimate of places,
as others share
their private thoughts.

Like early morning stoned
tattoo artists afraid
of dying before
understanding
how the ocean's
bed is made.

Like lonely new
teens who purge
and sing beautiful words,
and artists who cut pain
into their skin,
as if crying is a sin.

I am alone at the door,
but it is the humanity
I see

when I keep my eye
to the peephole.

Words Among Us

If words
are my religion
then Verless
is my preacher.

It ain't what
you think either,
I mean
he is a helluva poet,
but the world
is flush with
helluva poets.

Maybe,
more
the way he
looks when
he mentions
his woman or

spends time
with his kids
wrapped in
blankets,
watching t.v..

It's his
Damascus road
thing- shedding
skin
and more in
that change,
transformed.

The way he
remembers
the pain and
shares it,
forgiving his
trespassers,
even his

own transgressions.

Those are
the hardest
to forget.

It's the hope
I feel, the chance
for redemption
for the sins
of my father,

the sins of my own.

It is for
that bearded jesus
thing that he does,
love for
the tax collectors,
the hookers, and
the drunks-

and most
of the other
cabbies.

Maybe he is the
thief on the right
and I am
all that is left

and sometimes
all I have left
is his faith.

So that
kind of makes him
my preacher,

and if words
are my church,
then this

is kind of

my prayer -

help me

learn to forgive,

like Verless.

Undone

I took it
out again,
set it up
on an easel,
sure that
I wanted to
finish like so
many other
times.

I started it
long ago,
the citrus tones
and asian style
reminded me
how deeply
I had felt.

Shadow Man

and his guitar,
the beauty
of the
Willow World,
silent and in
pain, the two
of them
unsure how to
carry on.

The layers of
painted over
versions of them
would tell
the real tale
if
they could.

At first
they had looked
and longed

for each other
across canvas,
maybe he
more
than her
but still...

Then hurt,
Shadow began
to leave,
and the geisha
watched
sad,
unable to be his,
a tear
as she watched
him go.

Later,
she is painted
in white-

in mourning-
but her
back is turned
to him. She looks
back at the
castle
where she lives
as royalty,
he climbs
the same hill,
his progress
slow
and unsteady.

I would that
I could finish it,
I am unable.

I get it out
and set it
on easel

again,
on this day
you are wed,
and I look
at it.

I look at
you

I look at
me

at the way
I would have
things be,
and I wish
I could have
been more
graceful
in the letting go,
I lay aside

my brush
but I leave
the painting.

It remains undone,
but I will never finish
and it will always remain.

Maybe Better

The second

time I saw her

she walked

into my room

and saw

the mattress

on the floor

and said Jesus

Christ

you still live

like a hobo.

She threw

down

a canvas

messenger

bag filled with

protest pamphlets,

and porn from

Holland and
poems by
Baudelaire

then kicked
off her shoes,
Tom's,
and pulled
a shapeless
cotton dress
up and over
her head
and slipped
into bed next
to me.

Twenty and three
my junior
her skin was
cream and goodness
her hair

the color of
an Irish girl
named Maggie's,
her eyes of green
had already
given up
tears.

Do you have a drink?
she asked
and I passed
her what I had.
I am not
like the others,
she said,
not sad
or lonely

I am a writer,
a poet,

like you,
but better.
It was the closest
I had been to loving
in a long time.

We wrote a hell
of a story
before she
moved on.
She was a writer
and maybe
a little broken,

like me,
maybe better.

Them Bones

He was my
ace boon,
my number one
running buddy-
he was my biggest
fan, no one
enjoyed my
antics more.

We drove
stolen cars at
breakneck speeds
when I was a kid.
We played drinking
games with quarters
and fatal bravado,
jumped from windows
of other mens wives.

We walked dangerous
streets all night long.

We shot dope.

His company became
familiar and I resented
him but who else
was willing to
rattle the bones.
I gambled with him
and he ate sleeves
of crackers and said
that I looked
like shit.

Right back atcha.

And while Death

swept saltine crumbs

from his lap I switched

the dice

and made my

point

the hard way.

He was my friend but

it ain't cheatin'

if he don't see.

Dream Lovers Die

We were headed
to see the art
a couple of blocks
over, the first
time I rode in
her car.

What kind of music,

she asked and
without a thought
of how cool she was
or even the difference
in our ages I said,

Hillbilly.

She put in some Townes
and I fell in something
with her right then.

Prayer

I don't believe
in god
but I'd really
like to,
and I often get
a sort of
magic feeling
at sun-up
if I'm alive
and sober,
so damn
reassuring
still.

I try not to
worry
about if
there is or
if
there ain't,

but it pisses me
off - if you're
the daddy why
then so many
hungry
crying kids.
Worse.

My Granny
loved Jesus
and I reckon
most everybody
else
but he don't
make them like
her
anymore and if
he were real,
he
would.

I can't believe

in believe
in heaven but
it's been hell on
Earth since I
strayed from
Daddy's preachin'
and that heavy
leather
book.

I don't believe
in nothing but
I don't mind
my momma
praying
so long as it makes
her feel good,
she prays for me
and it don't
hurt
none.

www.ingramcontent.com/pod-product-compliance
Lightning Source LLC
LaVergne TN
LVHW041545070426
835507LV00011B/930